CONTENTS

PICASSO SELF PORTRAIT

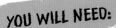

Picasso created weird and wonderful portraits. Here's how to make your own!

1 On tracing paper, draw a face-on portrait of yourself in pencil. Trace over a photograph of yourself or use a mirror.

2 On another piece of tracing paper, draw another portrait of yourself at the same size – this time from a profile view.

3 Draw a third portrait of yourself on another sheet of tracing paper at the same size – this time from a three-quarter turned view.

4 Take all three of your portraits and layer them on top of each other. Through the tracing paper, you should be able to see all three drawings. Line them up so your head is in the same place in each one.

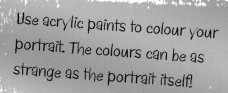

5 On a piece of cartridge paper, transfer your portraits (see page 31), picking out the different features to make a 'muddled' portrait. Thicken the lines you want to stand out.

Use acrylic paints to colour your portrait. The colours can be as strange as the portrait itself!

COLOUR WHEEL RUBBING

Explore the colours in a colour wheel with this rainbow design.

1 Collect some leaves from your garden or local park. Make sure they are different sizes and have some interesting patterns and textures.

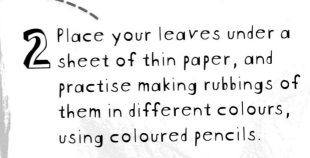

2 Place your leaves under a sheet of thin paper, and practise making rubbings of them in different colours, using coloured pencils.

6

3 Next, arrange six similar-sized leaves in a fanned circle. Lay a clean sheet of paper on top and rub over the leaves in the colours of the colour wheel. These colours are: red, orange, yellow, green, blue and purple.

4 Using the watercolour paints and a paintbrush, practise blending out the six colours, so they go from bold to faint. Use more paint to make the colours bold and more water to make them fainter.

5 Finish your colour wheel by applying this painting technique around your leaf circle. Blend the different colours together when they meet to make new shades and tones.

Use this picture for colour reference when painting other projects.

EASTER CHICK GIFTCARD

Combine painting and collage to make a bold design for a giftcard

1 On a piece of cardboard, draw an Easter chick design using simple shapes. Make sure your design will fit on an A5 piece of paper.

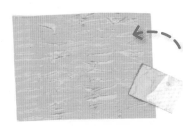

Yellow acrylic, with gold metallic paint dabbed over the surface using a small strip of card

Orange and yellow acrylic mixed together to make a bold orange

A dark violet for adding strong details

2 On a separate piece of card, experiment with different colours of paint to decide how to colour your chick design.

Violet and white acrylic to make a pale purple

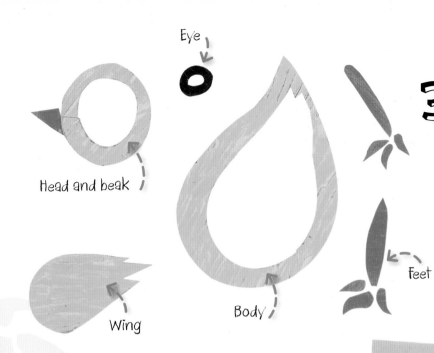

Eye

Head and beak

Wing

Body

Feet

3 Choose your favourite paint colours to paint the shapes of your chick. Once the paint is dry, cut these pieces out with scissors.

4 Assemble your pieces on your folded A4 cardboard. You can also add a background and a border decoration. Glue all the pieces into place.

You can make painted collage giftcards for any occassion! How about this scary pumpkin design?

9

DOODLE PAINTINGS

Doodling can free your imagination. You can get even more creative by painting the shapes you make.

1 Take your piece of paper and fineliner pen, and doodle a random line all around your paper. The line can circle, curl or zig-zag – anything you want!

2 When you've finished, look for pictures you could make from the shapes. If you look closely, this doodle could look like a duck and a mushroom.

3 Using your pen, fill in some extra details on the pictures you see in your doodle.

4 When you feel confident enough, paint your doodle picture to really bring it to life! You can experiment with your paints on a separate piece of paper first.

Every doodle you draw will make a new and exciting picture!

CREATE A MONSTER

Get imaginative with this monster character! Colouring with wax and paint can make great patterns.

1 To sketch out your monster character, draw egg shapes to make up the body, legs, arms and head.

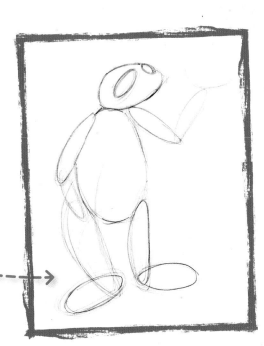

2 Link them together and add details, such as fingers, toes, horns and facial features. You could even make him hairy!

3 Before you add colour to your monster, experiment on a separate piece of paper. Take a candle and draw patterns and textures that you'd like to use on your monster. Paint over the wax patterns with watercolour paint. The patterns you drew should come through.

4 Draw the wax patterns on your monster. Think about what patterns you want him to have on different parts of his body. Paint your monster with watercolour paints.

5 Finally, use a black fineliner pen to add definition and detail to your monster. You can even add a fantastic background!

Turn the page to the next project to give your monster a friend!

13

MONSTER PETS

In the last project you created your own monster. Now keep him company with a cool monster pet!

YOU WILL NEED:

- Cartridge paper
- HB pencil
- Acrylic paints, in various colours
- Textured materials to paint with, such as fabric, sponge and tinsel
- Paintbrush
- Paint palette
- Black fineliner

1 Begin by drawing egg shapes to make different characters. Use your imagination – they can look like whatever you want them to!

2 Work up these shapes, adding fur, scales, toes, eyes and antennae – anything you want!

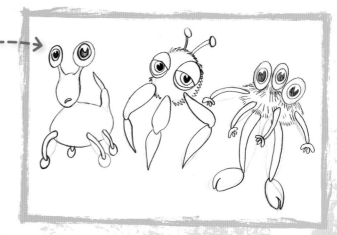

14

3 Before you add colour to your monster pets, take a clean sheet of paper and experiment with different effects. Try painting with other things besides a paintbrush. These could be things like fabric, your fingers or sponges. Apply a small amount of paint to them and press or dab them onto the paper.

fabric textures

fingerprints

tinsel

sponge

4 Choose your favourite painting techniques and use them to colour your monster pets. Think about what textures your different pets would have, depending on what features they have.

5 Finally, use a black fineliner pen to add definition and detail to your monster pets.

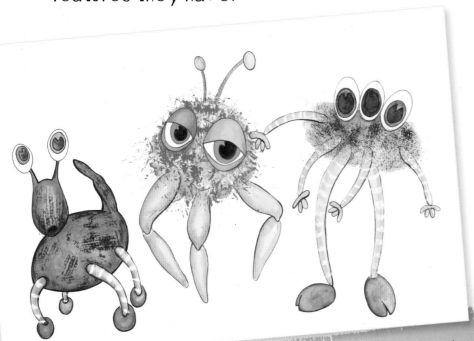

There's no limit to what your monster creations can look like!

15

GLOWING FISH

Using this unique painting technique, this colourful fish appears to almost glow.

1 First practise drawing fish shapes. Use rounded diamond shapes for the bodies and triangle shapes for the tails. Practise adding details, such as eyes, mouths, fins and scales.

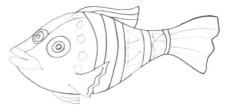

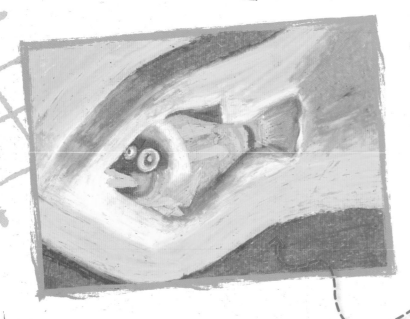

2 Draw your final big fish on your thick paper, then colour the fish and background using oil pastels and pressing very hard. Make it as colourful as possible and cover the entire paper. On a separate piece of paper, colour in a solid, smaller rectangle. This will be your test piece.

3 Take your black ready-made paint and paintbrush, and paint over your oil-pastel fish design. Cover the entire page, but leave a fine outline, so you can see where your fish drawing is. Paint over your test piece too. Let the paint dry completely.

4 On your test piece, use your sharp object to scratch away at the paint to reveal the colours underneath. Experiment scratching out different patterns, using different tools to get different effects. Here are some suggested pattern ideas. Be very careful with anything you use that is sharp.

5 Now scratch into your fish picture. If you feel confident enough, you can add more fish to make a full ocean scene.

Be careful not to scratch so hard that you go through the paper!

STENCIL SNOWFLAKES

Stencils are a fun and easy way to make loads of different patterns with paint.

1 Using the cups, draw two circles on a piece of thick paper. Cut the circles out, fold them in half, then fold them in half again.

2 On each of the folded circles, draw a different design. Cut out the shapes and unfold your circles.

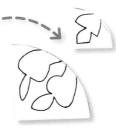

3 Using sticky tack, stick your stencils to your cartridge paper. Lightly dip a cotton bud into the paint and dab all over the stencils. Peel the stencils off and wait for the paint to dry before adding more.

4 Ask an adult to help you with the spray paint. You must make sure you are in a large room with an open window or outside. Layer the stencils however you like. Stick your pencils to the paper, as before, and spray a light coat of paint over the top.

5 Layer your stencils any way you want. You can even stick them onto your painting afterwards for collage effect.

There are so many different shapes you can meake with circle stencils.

PERSONALIZED BOOKMARK

Use the initials of your name to make a funky design for a bookmark.

YOU WILL NEED:

- HB pencil
- Two sheets of thick card
- Ruler
- Scissors
- Watercolour paints
- Paint palette
- Small paintbrush

1 On your card, draw two horizontal lines 5 cm apart. Write your initials between these lines. Use a ruler to help you.

2 Using your ruler again, make the letters thick and chunky.

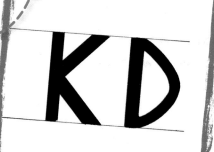

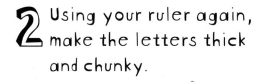

3 Using scissors, cut these letters out. You will use them as stencils for your bookmark.

4 From your other sheet of card, cut out a strip 5.5 cm wide and 23 cm long. Use your stencils to create an interesting pattern on your bookmark. You can even flip them around and use them back to front.

5 Using watercolour paints, paint your bookmark using bright, complementary colours. Either yellow and purple, red and green, or blue and orange. Cut it out with scissors.

By arranging your initials in different ways, you can make bookmarks that have different shapes and patterns.

AMAZING MOSAIC

Create your own coloured and textured mosaics to make a cool mosaic design.

Paint mixed with sand

Thin paint applied with large brush

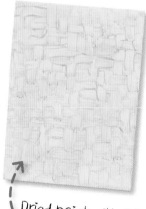

Dried paint with PVA glue patterns applied on top

Paint mixed with glitter

Paint swirled into patterns with fingertip

1 On the sheets of card, create different coloured or textured backgrounds. You can add sand or glitter to give the paint texture, or use your fingers or a sponge to make patterns. Let them dry completely.

Paint dabbed onto paper with small sponge

2 Using scissors, cut your coloured backgrounds into pieces. Try to cut them into shapes that will fit together easily, such as squares, rectangles and trianges. Make sure the largest pieces are no more than 4 x 4 cm.

3 On a large sheet of cartridge paper, draw a 24 x 24 cm grid, and divide it up by 4 cm x 4 cm squares.

4 Now get creative! Make a mosaic pattern by gluing the shapes onto the grid.

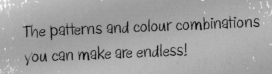

The patterns and colour combinations you can make are endless!

FRAMED SUNSET

YOU WILL NEED:

- Picture frame
- Pictures of sunsets for inspiration
- Large paintbrushes
- Acrylic paint, in various colours
- Paint palette

The artist Howard Hodgkin uses large brushes and sweeping brushstrokes to make paintings that look like sunsets.

1 Ask an adult to remove the glass from the picture frame, so you are left with the frame and backing only.

2 Look at your sunset pictures and decide on the background colours to paint your frame. Use large, horizontal brushstrokes to paint sweeping colour across the frame.

3 Once dry, choose other colours from your sunset pictures to layer over the background. Add these colours using the same sweeping brushstrokes.

4 Keep on layering colours until you are happy with your sunset. Remember to keep the brushstrokes loose and flowing.

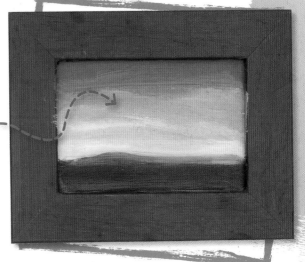

5 Wait until your frame is completely dry before hanging on the wall!

Search on the Internet for 'Howard Hodgkin' to see beautiful sunset paintings just like yours!

PATCHWORK LANDSCAPE

Countryside landscapes can look a lot like patchwork. This inspired the artist David Hockney to make really colourful paintings.

YOU WILL NEED:

- Picture of countryside fields, for inspiration
- Masking tape
- Large piece of paper
- HB pencil
- Acrylic paints
- Paintbrush
- Paint palette
- Cotton buds

1 Look at your countryside picture and plan out your patchwork fields using light pencil lines. Stick lengths of masking tape around the edges of the paper. This will keep your painting neat.

Foreground

Middle

Background

2 Look carefully at the colours in your contryside picture. What shades would be best to use for the foreground, middle and background? Do the colours get paler as they move into the distance? Experiment with the colours you would like to use.

Grass: long, thin brush, dabbed onto paper on its side

Hedges: painting with a cotton bud

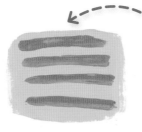

Cornfields: bold red and yellow stripes

3 On a separate sheet of paper, experiment with the brushstrokes you can make to suggest different parts of the landscape.

4 Paint your landscape, one patchwork square at a time. Use your experiments to decide what colours and techniques to apply to each area.

5 Finally, once your painting is dry, peel off the masking tape.

You could even paint the scene outside your window.

MATERIALS

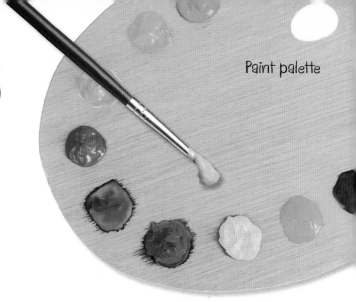

Paint palette

Drawing pencils

An HB pencil is recommend to begin with and then try B and 2B for softer shading. Don't try to shade with an H pencil as it is too hard.'H' pencils get harder as the numbers go up, and 'B' pencils get softer at the numbers go up.

Coloured pencils

Coloured pencils come in a huge variety of colours. Generally they are similar in hardness, but soft ones that can be smudged and blended are available too.

Watercolour pencils

Watercolour pencils look very similar to normal coloured pencils, but they are soluable in water, which will give your

Coloured pencils

drawings a watercolour effect. You can either dip them in water before drawing or colour as normal and then brush water over the top.

Pens and markers

To add detail to a dry painting, try fineliners in sizes 0.1mm, 0.3mm, 0.5mm, 0.7mm. For thicker marks try markers with broader nibs.

Permanent Markers are generally resistant to paint but won't wash off most surfaces so you have to be very careful with them.

Paper

Cartridge Paper is an excellent choice for pencil and acrylic paints. It comes in different thicknesses. The thicker versions will withstand being painted.

Watercolour paper is paper specially designed for watercolour paints. It has a wonderful texture that is perfect for the delicacy of watercolour painting.

Acrylic paint

Acrylic paint comes in tubes. It is quite thick and a little can go a long way, so only use small amount. You can thin it with water, but the colours are more vibrant if you use it without. When acrylic paint dries, you cannot lift it off with water. It can only be painted over. It has a glue-like surface, once dry, that is waterproof.

Watercolour paints

Watercolour paints can bought as blocks with a palette or in small tubes. If you buy tubes, only squeeze a small amount onto a palette and mix with water. If using blocks, wet a paintbrush and stroke over the block and paint onto a palette. The more water you use, the lighter the colour. If you want a very intense colour, use only a little water, just enough to lift the colour from the block.

Paintbrushes

Paintbrushes come in many different shapes and sizes – round or flat, thick or thin. Use the right type of paintbrush for the kind of painting you are doing. Small paintbrushes are ideal for adding detail and large, flat brushes are good for big, sweeping strokes. Clean brushes after you use them and they will last for a long time.

Materials to add texture

Sponge

Texture can be added to paint using many different methods. Try mixing things like sand and glitter into your paint. You can add texture using PVA glue, letting it dry and painting over the top. You can also paint with other tools besides paintbrushes, like sponges, cotton buds and even your fingers!

Glitter

TECHNIQUES

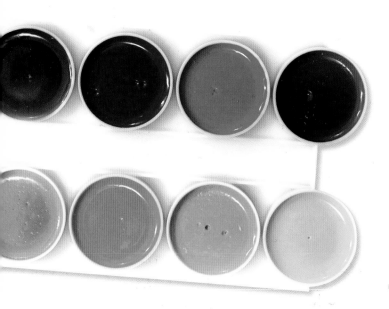

Using watercolour

To apply colour, use light colours first, then build up to darker colours. Let the paint dry before adding more, unless you want the colours to bleed and mix together.

If you paint a colour onto paper, but decide you want it lighter, you can add water with a paintbrush to lift the paint off.

It is a good idea to use thick paper with watercolours, as you tend to use more water. Paper can only take so much water before it begins to break up.

Using acrylic

To mix colours, always start with the lightest colour on the palette. Add a little of the darker colour at a time, until you are happy with the colour you have mixed.

When painting, think about the direction of your strokes. Sometimes you can see the marks of brush hairs moving in a direction. Also think about the length of your strokes. Do you want long, sweeping strokes or quick, short flicks?

Using pencils

When drawing, use a light pressure on your pencil. If your pencil marks are too dark they may show through or mix with the paint. If pencil marks are too dark, simply use an eraser to lighten them before painting.

Adding texture

To add a grainy texture, mix a small amount of sand or glitter with your paint before use.

To add a pattern, texture or design with PVA glue, apply the PVA in the pattern or texture you want, allow it to dry completely and then paint over the top. PVA glue often comes in a squeezy bottle with a nozzle to make this easier.

To apply paint with a sponge, a cotton bud or fabric, dip the item into a small amount of paint and then dab it onto paper.

Wax painting

When you paint on top of wax with a thin water-based paint, such as watercolour, an interesting effect happens. Because the paint cannot stick to the wax, you will be able to see the wax drawing through the paint. You can use a candle to draw with before applying the paint, but remember you won't be able to see what you are drawing! You can also use coloured wax crayons to achieve this effect.

Transferring a tracing

To transfer a tracing on tracing paper onto paper, turn the tracing paper onto its back and carefully draw over the lines in pencil. Next, flip the tracing paper back onto the right side and lay a sheet of paper underneath it. Carefully draw over the tracing with a heavy pressure on your pencil. The tracing should now have transferred onto the paper.

Sgraffito

With this technique you can scratch through paint to reveal a layer of colour underneath. Apply blocks of bold colour to thick paper with oil pastels, then apply a thick layer of ready-made paint over the top. Once dry, carefully scratch the paint away with a sharp object.

INDEX